Every
CROWN
Has
a
Story

Marya Patrice Sherron

Every CROWN Has a Story

An Imprint of KI Productions, LLC

Printed in the United States of America
ISBN: 978-1-961605-10-7

First Edition

Written, Designed, & Edited by Marya Patrice Sherron

Support the Crown Act
& Stay Informed

Senator Holly J. Mitchell was the first to introduce The CROWN Act (Senate Bill 188) in the state of California, the first state to sign the bill into law. New York was the second state to introduce the CROWN Act under the leadership of Assemblywoman Tremaine Wright (D-Bedford-Stuyvesant, Northern Crown Heights) and Senator Jamaal Bailey (D-Bronx, Westchester), and Governor Cuomo signed the CROWN Act into law on July 12th, deeming the legislation effective immediately. New Jersey became the third state to enact the CROWN Act.

State Senator Sandra Cunningham (District 31) and Assembly woman Angela McKnight (District 31) championed the legislation and Governor Phil Murphy signed the CROWN Act into law on December 19th, the one-year anniversary of the wrestling match where New Jersey high school wrestler Andrew Johnson's locs were forcibly cut off. The states of Virginia, Colorado, Washington, Maryland, Connecticut, Delaware, Nevada, Maine, Tennessee, Massachusetts, and Minnesota have also enacted the CROWN Act. Additional bills were signed in New Mexico, Nebraska, Oregon, Illinois, Louisiana, and Alaska that were inspired by The CROWN Act. In addition, the CROWN Act has become law in forty-four (44) municipalities.

In March 2021, the federal bill H.R 2116 was introduced in the U.S. House of Representatives by Congresswoman Bonnie Watson Coleman (D-NJ) and S.888 was introduced in the U.S. Senate by Senator Cory Booker. On March 18, 2022, the federal CROWN Act bill passed in the House of Representatives with a vote of 235 Yeas and 189 Nays.

On December 14, 2022, the federal bill was brought to the Senate floor for passage by unanimous consent. Unfortunately, the bill did not receive a vote in the Senate. The federal CROWN Act will now need to be reintroduced in the 2023 legislative session.

Introduction

Hair is quite literally the narrative thread linking the fibers of my very being together. My hair has always been an extension of my views, emotions, and political agency. This meant that each hair-season had a story.

I designed "Every Crown Has a Story" with this belief in mind. Our hair-stories are rich; they are art; and, they chronicle our growth in unexpected ways.

Hair carries timeless global connotations and has been a constant source by which beauty is measured and assigned. Yet, very little has been done with regard to the cultural meaning and conversations surrounding hair politics and policy and the ways in which we are influenced by each. The Hair Chronicles series is committed to this discourse and documenting the artistic expressions of such.

What are your hair stories?

Consider working through this book with a group, conduct weekly virtual calls; work through it with your mother or daughter, or on your own. The structure & prompts will work in every setting. On your own, follow your natural flow and work at your own pace. As a group, consider doing one section a week for ten weeks and encourage participants to complete 2 of the prompts for each meeting.

The most important thing is that you make this Your Own! There are no right or wrong answers or right or wrong ways to start. Jump around or work in order. Start, stop, reflect. Color, draw, sketch. Write in prose, poetry, or use bullets. Tape photos or glue a collage to your doodle and note pages. Make it 100% Your Own!

... Just make sure you Tell Your Story. No yes or no responses. Be descriptive — use imagery and all the details you can remember. Take us there with you on the page and into the moment you are telling.

In the end, I hope you laugh out loud, shed healthy tears, and walk away knowing that your story matters too.

XOXO
Marya

This Crown Belongs to:

_____

My Hair Timeline

Note your shifts over the years. Come back & add to your timeline as you work through each section..

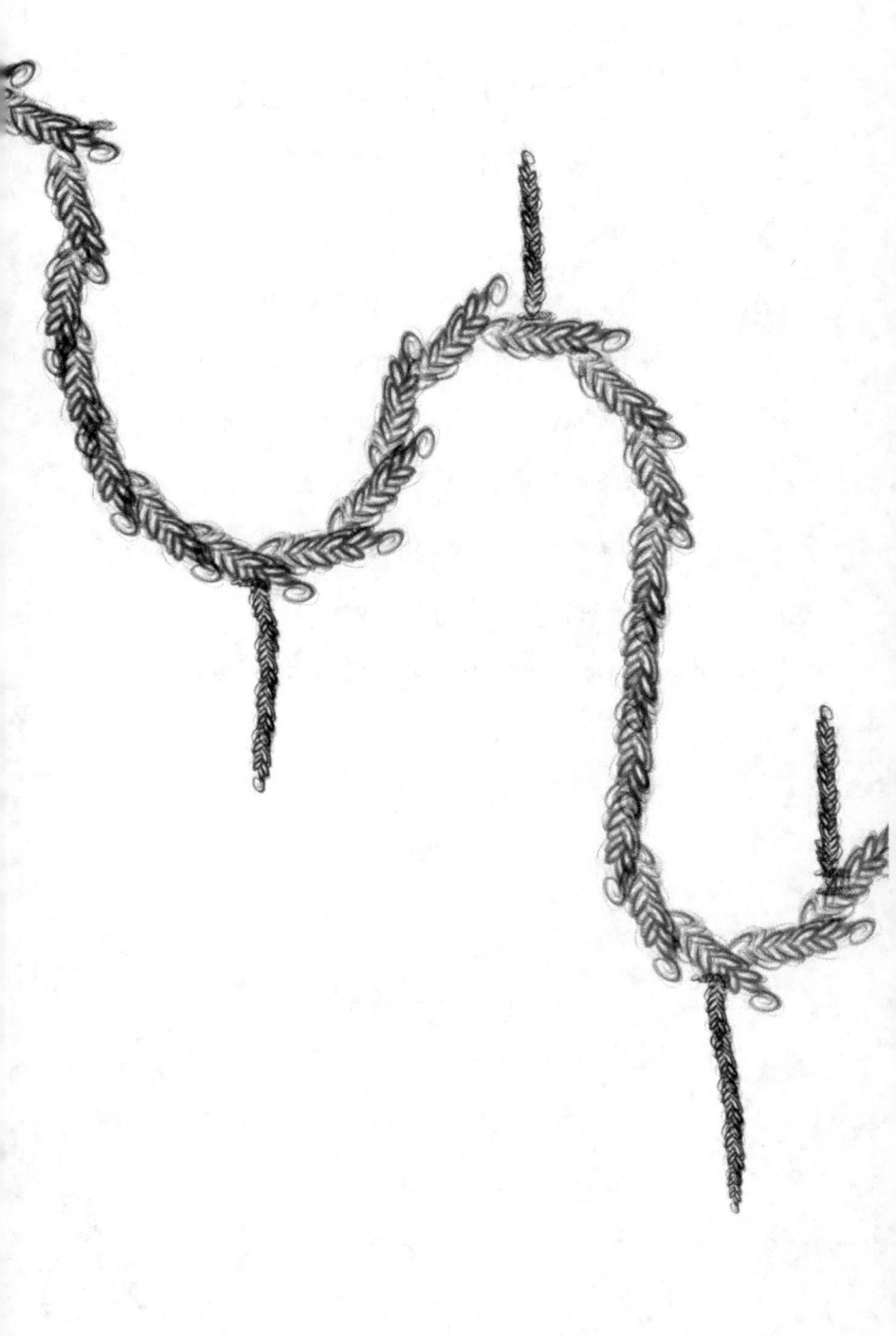

Prompts About
Your Roots

(birth -12)

When did you first notice hair? What caused you to notice it?

Describe hair notions in your upbringing?

What is your earliest hair memory?

When did you start doing your own hair?

Did you have a signature (a cut, style, or accessory)?

Any picture Day memories to share?

Did you have a favorite style and/or one you detested?

_____

_____

_____

_____

_____

_____

_____

_____

_____

_____

_____

_____

_____
_____
_____
_____
_____
_____
_____
_____
_____
_____
_____
_____
_____

What took your attention from this section or from your group
discussion... or you can just doodle.

Prompts About Youth

Describe the first memory that comes to mind in this age range.

What styles do you remember wearing?

What were popular styles?

Did you have a signature (a cut, style, or accessory)?

Which of your friends had the most memorable styles?

Did music videos or entertainers impact your hair choices?

_____

_____

_____

_____

_____

_____

_____

_____

_____

_____

_____

_____

_____

_____

_____

_____

_____

_____

_____

_____

_____

_____

_____

_____

_____

_____

_____

_____

_____

_____

_____

_____

_____

_____

_____

_____

_____

_____

_____

_____

What took your attention from this section or from your group discussion... or you can just doodle.

Prompts About
Influencers & Inspirations

Who was the first person that influenced your hair styles?

Who do you admire because of their hair choices?

Have you ever cut or styled your hair like a celebrity?

What role have trends played in your hair styles?

What or who comes to mind when you think of Music and hair?

What or who comes to mind when you think of Bold and Hair?

_____

_____

_____

_____

_____

_____

_____

_____

_____

_____

_____

_____

_____

_____

_____

_____

_____

_____

_____

_____

_____

_____

_____

_____

_____

_____

_____
_____
_____
_____
_____
_____
_____
_____
_____
_____
_____
_____
_____

What took your attention from this section or from your group
discussion... or you can just doodle.

Prompts for Fun

Have you ever experimented with colors? Describe the colors, styles, and if there was an occasion.

Describe a favorite costume & how your styled your hair or wig.

How do you style your hair when you're in a fun, silly mood?

What are your favorite accessories to jazz up your hair?

_____

_____

_____

_____

_____

_____

_____

_____

_____

_____

_____

_____

_____

_____

_____

_____

_____

_____

_____

_____

_____

_____

_____

_____

_____

_____

_____

_____

_____

_____

_____

_____

_____

_____

_____

_____

_____

_____

_____

What took your attention from this section or from your group
discussion... or you can just doodle.

Prompts for Occasions

What is your favorite Little Black Dress & Black Tie hair style?

Describe your prom, graduation or wedding hair.

Describe your hair on a lounge-around the house day.

Describe your hair style for a job interview, date, or girls night out.

_____

_____

_____

_____

_____

_____

_____

_____

_____

_____

_____

_____

_____

What took your attention from this section or from your group discussion... or you can just doodle.

Prompts for Life-Changing Seasons

What immediately comes to mind when you think of life-changing seasons?

Explore the topics below that grab you:

Graduations or New Positions

Marriage or Divorce

Parenthood/Pregnancy

Empty-Nester

Becoming a Grandparent

Becoming an Aunt/Uncle or God-Parent

Loss

Travel or Relocation

_____

_____

_____

_____

_____

_____

_____

_____

_____

_____

_____

_____

_____

What took your attention from this section or from your group
discussion... or you can just doodle.

Prompts About
Your Process

What is your hair process & routine today?

How has your process changed over the years?

What are your favorite products?

Imagine you can only bring three hair items/products with you on an island for a month, what would you bring and why?

Do you eat particular foods for your hair (for example, salmon, blueberries, and walnuts are said to stimulate growth)?

Describe your gym, swim, or vacation hair styles or routines.

_____

_____

_____

_____

_____

_____

_____

_____

_____

_____

_____

_____

_____

_____

_____
_____
_____
_____
_____
_____
_____
_____
_____
_____
_____
_____
_____
_____

What took your attention from this section or from your group
discussion... or you can just doodle.

Prompts for Self-Discovery

Are there times you styled your hair in a way your spirit rejected. but you did it for someone else or out of obligation?

How do you style your hair that makes you feel light and free-spirited?

What old photo makes you smile & why?

What is a style you are least likely to ever wear Or an accessory you will not likely use?

Who is that last person you offered a hair compliment to?

Is there a question you do not like to be asked regarding your hair or process?

How do you feel about your crown today?

[How] Does your hair converge with your identity?

Explore the role of others in your hair style choices (this requires you to look at what the opinions of others means to you).

[How] Has your creativity & imagination revealed itself in your styles?

Have you fallen in love with your hair? If not. what are your obstacles?

What took your attention from this section or from your group discussion... or you can just doodle.

Prompts for Healing

Some wounds run deep and deserve more
attention than this book will allow. Please listen
to yourself and honor your needs. If you have more
to unpack, consider seeking a suitable therapist.
Our mental & emotional health must be a
priority.

Do you have hair-hurts?

Describe a hair-mishap story or two.

Something said you have never quite forgotten.

Write a love letter to your hair.

Write a letter to you from the point-of-view of
your hair.

_____

_____

_____

_____

_____

_____

_____

_____

_____

_____

_____

_____

_____

What took your attention from this section or from your group
discussion... or you can just doodle.

Journal Prompts About the Future

Learn something new about hair in your family: Ask someone (a parent, child, sibling, or spouse) to share a hair-story or fun fact you don't already know.

Describe a daring hair change — one you want to try, but are apprehensive about.

Do you have any hair related fears?

How do you imagine you will style your hair in 5 years? 10 Years?

What is a hair trend you expect to see in the years ahead?

What are your thoughts on the future of the Crown Act?

What is a future hair product or accessory you hope to see?

_____

_____

_____

_____

_____

_____

_____

_____

_____

_____

_____

_____

_____

_____

_____

_____

_____

_____

_____

_____

_____

_____

_____

_____

_____

_____

What took your attention from this section or from your group
discussion... or you can just doodle.